In memory of my father

I also dedicate this book to my grandchildren: Tyler, Anna, Eida and Ella.

And to all children. They all deserve to be loved.

All rights reserved

Text and Illustrations © 2018 Ruth Lieberherr

Book Layout & Design by CVaughanDesigns.com

ISBN: 978-1-7328877-3-2

Printed in the United States

The Boy Without A Name

Ruth Lieberherr

"Grandma, look what I found! Who is the boy in the picture?"

"Dear Anna. He is your great-grandfather. Here in the photo he is a little boy who is three years old."

"Just like me. Why is he so sad?"

"That is a long story," Grandma replied.

"Please, please, tell me this story!" pleaded Anna, snuggling in her grandma's lap.

So grandmother began.

A long time ago, in the country called Switzerland, a baby boy was born. His mother was young, poor, unmarried, and her family did not want to take care of the baby. So the baby was taken from her and given to a farmer and his family.

The mother was very sad without her baby. She hoped he would have enough to eat and a place to play wherever he was.

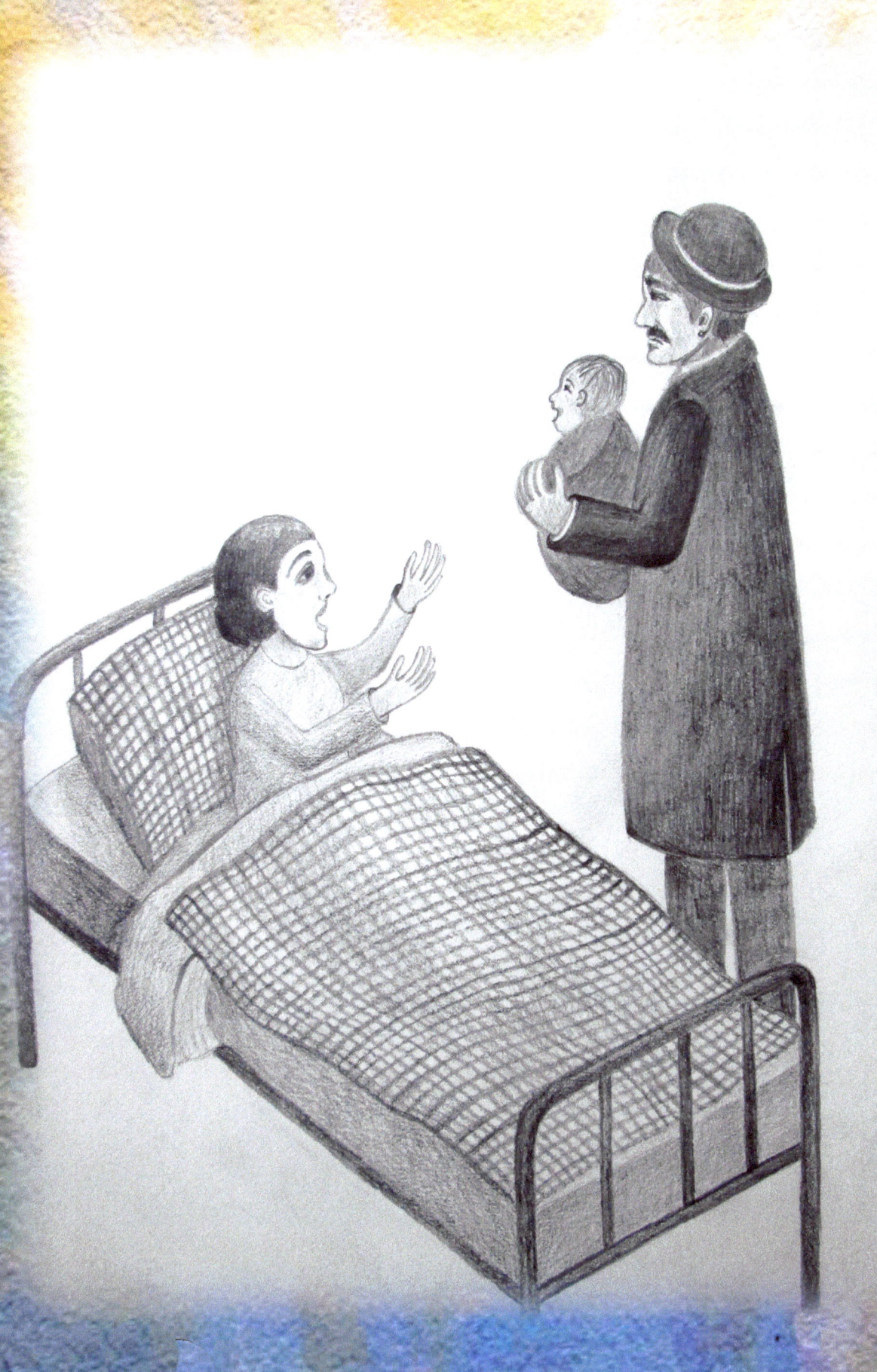

The baby's father who had grown up in an orphanage without a father or mother, could not keep the baby either. He also was young, poor and unmarried. But he worked long hours to help pay the farmer for the upkeep of the little boy.

The baby boy grew into a toddler. The farmer and his family just called him "the boy", although his parents had given him a good name. As soon as he was able, he had to work. Most people used horses in those days. The three year old boy was sent with a shovel and a pail to scoop up horse manure in the street and bring it back to the farm to fertilize the vegetable garden.

Sometimes the boy had to sleep in the barn, where he had his secret friends. He collected snails and sheltered them from the rain. When he was older he made little beds for orphaned mice and fed them crumbs of his own food. He also cared for birds that had fallen out of nests and nurtured them until they could fly.

A few times a man he did not know would come to visit and give him a small coin. But the boy was afraid of the stranger and did not know what to do with the money. Much later the boy found out that the stranger was his real father.

When the boy was older, his father married and was happy to take him into his home. The stepmother resented the boy because she had no children of her own.

But now the boy was called by his real name: Oscar!

He went to school and earned good grades. Oscar was a generous, hard-working boy and helped his stepmother with her laundry business at home. When he was fourteen, his father became disabled and lost his job. But his father's employer kindly hired Oscar as an apprentice. Oscar was glad he could provide for his parents and himself. He also got a good, practical education learning to install flour mills.

When Oscar finished his apprenticeship, he was sent to many countries to install the machinery for the flour mills which his employer sold all over the world. Oscar was proud of his work that helped to provide flour for many families to bake their bread. He enjoyed traveling and getting to know different people, customs and languages. He made friends in many countries. In addition to his native Swiss German he spoke French, Italian, Dutch, Swedish and even some Greek.

During a big war, Oscar could not travel home. He hoped to get married and have children. But his fiancée grew tired of waiting for him and married somebody else. Oscar was very disappointed when he found out, but nevertheless he was happy when he could finally come home. In Switzerland he helped to protect the country's border together with many other men. He worked with cannons and horses and helped with building a fortress inside a mountain.

After the war, Oscar met a beautiful teacher named Ida. They loved each other very much and soon were married. When Oscar was sent to another country for work, his wife Ida accompanied him.

In that far away land, they were both very joyful when a little boy was born to them. They named him Peter. A year later, Ida gave birth to a baby girl. They named her Ruth.

Oscar, Ida and their children returned home to Switzerland, where Oscar enjoyed being part of Ida's large family. He loved getting to know Ida's parents, her many sisters and brothers, their spouses and children. Ida taught school. Oscar took care of a big flour mill and an electric power plant that belonged to the mill. Peter and Ruth grew up next to the mill and their father's workshop.

Oscar was happy to help his children and their friends make wooden boats and to build forts behind his workshop. He kept apples, paper and pencils in the drawer of his workbench for the children to work on their own designs.

For a time, a tiny crippled mouse lived in Oscar's workshop. It nibbled on pieces of apple and cheese that Oscar shared with it while he worked on his workbench. And the children, too, loved to visit with the little mouse.

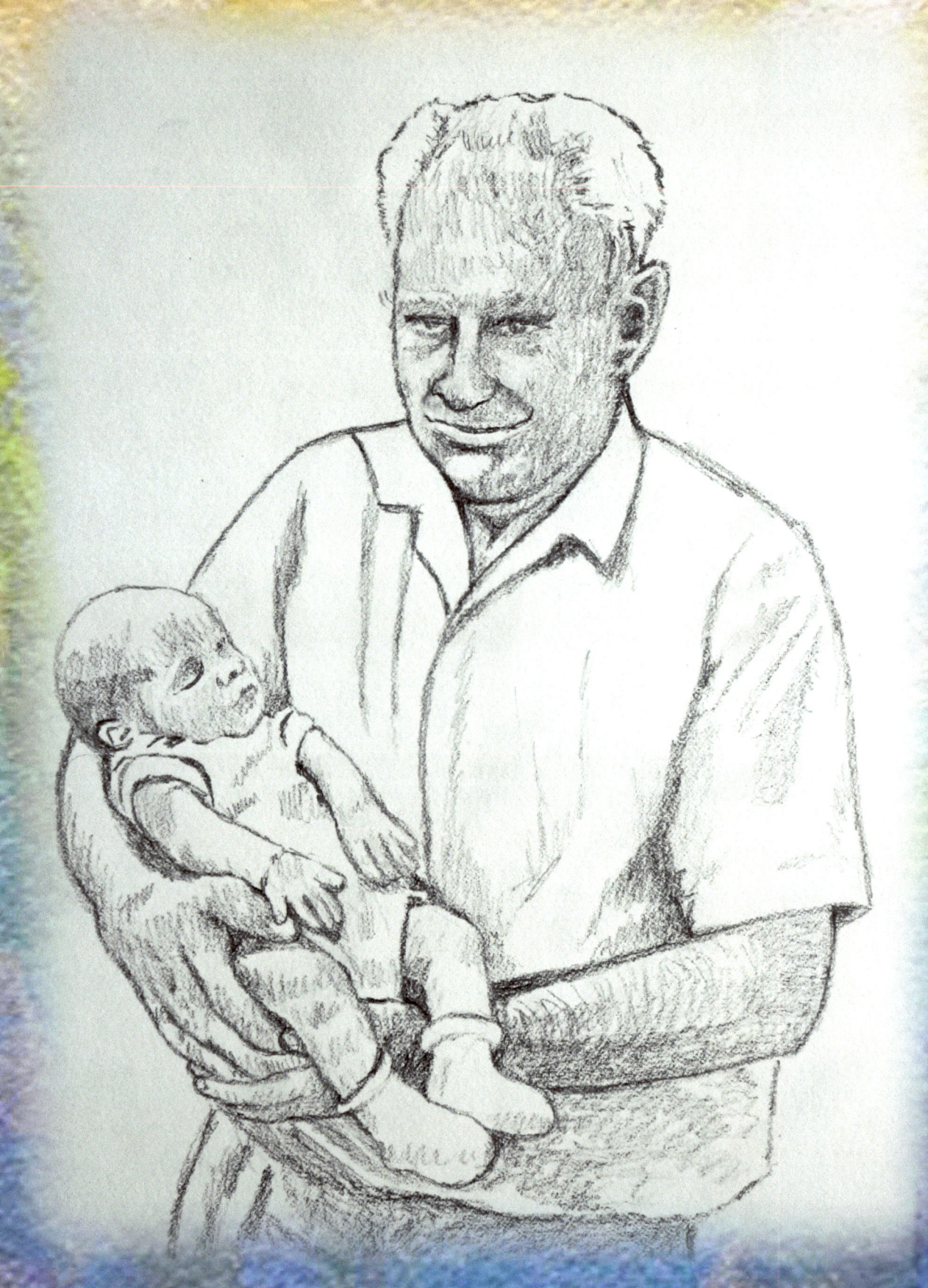

When Oscar's children grew up, they soon had children of their own. Oscar loved his grandchildren very much.

Oscar kept working. He enjoyed meeting new people. He liked children. He always was happy to help not only family and friends, but also strangers. He was glad to give back to those less fortunate, when he could.

After many years Oscar grew old and tired. One day, he did not wake up. His wife Ida, his children and grandchildren mourned his passing on. But many people came from nearby and far away to Oscar's memorial. They came to celebrate his long and caring life. Oscar had touched them all.

The boy without a name was honored by many people at his death. They all knew his true name.

Oscar

"Oh", smiled Anna and hugged her grandma.
"Dear Oscar! Now I know him too!"

Ruth's story

My father, Oscar Kübler (1907 - 1994) was among the many foster children/indentured child laborers (the "Verdingkinder") who were taken from unwed mothers or poor or troubled families and placed with farmers in Switzerland. Often they also were put in poor houses or orphanages. No matter where they were placed they usually received little food or love. They had to work hard and in many cases were beaten and treated meanly. Many of the children never got a proper education and had a hard time keeping a job as adults.

Though his childhood was a difficult one, my father Oscar was a cheerful, nurturing man, who did everything for my brother and me. He had received a good practical education and held a demanding and fulfilling job as an installer of flour mills ("Mühlebauer"). I think both his ability to connect with people and to hold down a demanding job was in part because his father (my grandfather Paul Oskar Kübler, 1885 - 1933), always cared about his welfare and was able to take Oscar into his home when he was about nine years old.

The stories my father told us were about his exciting adventures traveling and working in foreign countries. Only when he was dying, did he tell us about not knowing his mother, being called "the boy" on the farm, collecting manure as a three-year-old, and about the stranger, his father, who would visit him at the farm and give him a coin.

As I researched my father's life, I found the name and birth date of his mother (Marie Philomène Baudin, born 1886 in Vesin, in the French part of Switzerland), but unfortunately not much more about her and her family.

Ruth with a mobile she made about her father's life.

Ruth Lieberherr - Writer, Artist and Illustrator. She has written and illustrated the picturebook *The Caterpillar and the Butterfly* (*Die Raupe und der Schmetterling*). She also illustrated the following picturebooks: *Winter, Awake!* (author Linda Kroll), *Journey to Inner Space* (author Deborah R. Cohen), *The Knottles* (author Nancy Mellon), *Hafez, The Mathematical Stonecutter* (author Michael Punzak) and *By Some Great Spell* (author Mary Beth Melton). Her paintings are in private and corporate collections and are exhibited in galleries in the U.S. and Europe.

www.RuthLieberherr.com

www.ingramcontent.com/pod-product-compliance
Lightning Source LLC
Chambersburg PA
CBHW040735150426
42811CB00063B/1645